Facts About the White Faced Capuchin

By Lisa Strattin

© 2020 Lisa Strattin

FREE BOOK

Get a FREE copy HERE

LisaStrattin.com/Subscribe-Here

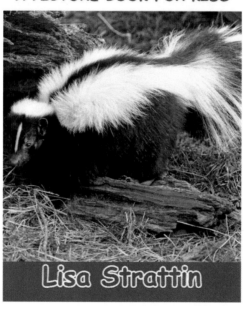

Facts for Kids Picture Books by Lisa Strattin

Little Blue Penguin, Vol 92

Chipmunk, Vol 5

Frilled Lizard, Vol 39

Blue and Gold Macaw, Vol 13

Poison Dart Frogs, Vol 50

Blue Tarantula, Vol 115

African Elephants, Vol 8

Amur Leopard, Vol 89

Sabre Tooth Tiger, Vol 167

Baboon, Vol 174

Sign Up for New Release Emails Here

http://LisaStrattin.com/subscribe-here

COVER IMAGE

https://www.flickr.com/photos/thejaan/14657902177/

ADDITIONAL IMAGES

https://www.flickr.com/photos/royluck/15011918612/

https://www.flickr.com/photos/31267353@N03/25463401660/

https://www.flickr.com/photos/thejaan/14657742440/

https://www.flickr.com/photos/briangratwicke/30744216246/

https://www.flickr.com/photos/thejaan/14844090532/

https://www.flickr.com/photos/67446336@N00/24080400776/

https://www.flickr.com/photos/royluck/14825760397/

https://www.flickr.com/photos/briangratwicke/22662802900/

https://www.flickr.com/photos/31267353@N03/43506825702/

https://www.flickr.com/photos/ekilby/9604894402/

Contents

INTRODUCTION

The White Faced Capuchin is also called the White Headed or White Throated Capuchin. They are medium-sized monkeys that live natively in Central and South America.

CHARACTERISTICS

The White Faced Capuchin is probably the best known and recognized species of monkey in the world. They are considered to be one of the most intelligent of all the monkeys!

If you ever see a real-life organ grinder, or pictures of one in a book, the monkey they have as their companion is usually a White Faced Capuchin.

They are not known as being territorial where they live because they move around as much as a mile or more every day!

APPEARANCE

The White Faced Capuchin is known because of their white head, throat and face! This is the distinctive characteristic that allows us to identify them at just a moment's glance. Other than that, they resemble other species of monkeys.

They are black, gray and brown, with the white markings on their face and have a long tail.

You know what a monkey looks like, don't you?

TROOP LIFE

The family-type group of around 20 different White Faced Capuchins is called a troop. In the family is a leading male, called the alpha male. His role is to make sure the troop is protected as well as to be a partner to the females by making more baby monkeys with them.

The alpha male is like the "Big Daddy" of the whole troop!

LIFE SPAN

In the wild, the White Faced Capuchin lives between 15 to 20 years. In captivity, they have been known to live over 50 years!

SIZE

The average adult White Faced Capuchin is between 3 and 4 feet tall and weighs less than 9 pounds!

HABITAT

The White Faced Capuchin lives in all kinds of forests all over Central and South America. They are not particular about any particular forest, just that there are lots of trees for them and plenty of food.

DIET

The White Faced Capuchin mostly eats berries and fruits, but also eats some frogs, small birds, insects and various plants.

They play an important part of keeping the forest alive and healthy because more plants grow when they drop the seeds from the fruits and berries they eat to the ground.

FRIENDS AND ENEMIES

The White Faced Capuchin is friends with those in their own troop, but when different troops come into contact with each other, they challenge each other. It doesn't really become a fight, but they do prefer to keep their troop separated from others.

Snakes and Eagles hunt and kill the White Faced Capuchin in their native jungle habitats.

SUITABILITY AS PETS

The White Faced Capuchin is a wonderful pet if you want to have a monkey as a pet. They do need a lot of attention and like to play, so you have to be willing to spend time with one if you choose to have one as a pet.

They are trainable and lovable, but they can have a bit of a crazy, wild streak.

There are veterinarians who are capable of helping you keep your monkey healthy, but you should check to make sure there is one who knows about them close to where you live, just in case you need medical care for your pet.

COLOR ME

COLOR ME

Please leave me a review here:

http://lisastrattin.com/Review-Vol-374

For more Kindle Downloads Visit Lisa Strattin
Author Page on Amazon Author Central

http://amazon.com/author/lisastrattin

To see upcoming titles, visit my website at
LisaStrattin.com– all books available on kindle!

http://lisastrattin.com

FREE BOOK

FOR ALL SUBSCRIBERS – SIGN UP NOW

FOR MY SPAM-FREE NEWSLETTER

LisaStrattin.com/Subscribe-Here

FACTS ABOUT THE
SKUNK

A PICTURE BOOK FOR KIDS

Lisa Strattin

Made in the USA
Las Vegas, NV
22 February 2021